AGRICULTURE

Troll Associates

AGRICULTURE

by Louis Sabin

Illustrated by Joseph Veno

Troll Associates

Library of Congress Cataloging in Publication Data

Sabin, Louis.
   Agriculture.

   Summary: Traces the history of agriculture, which is
the science of cultivating the soil, producing crops, and
raising livestock, from prehistoric farming to modern
agribusiness.
      1. Agriculture—Juvenile literature.   [1. Agriculture—
History.   2. Farms—History]   I. Veno, Joseph, ill.
II. Title.
S519.S17   1984   630   84-2710
ISBN 0-8167-0204-7 (lib. bdg.)
ISBN 0-8167-0205-5 (pbk.)

10 9 8 7 6 5 4 3 2 1

Agriculture is the science of cultivating the soil, producing crops, and raising livestock. It is a rice paddy in China or a cattle ranch in Argentina. It is a wheat field in North America and a coffee plantation in Brazil.

Agriculture is raising dairy cows for their milk and cheese or raising sheep for their wool and meat. It is a scientific poultry farm, a fish hatchery, a mink ranch. It's a cotton plantation, fields of pineapples, and groves of oranges, lemons, and limes. In short, agriculture is farming of all kinds.

Civilization depends on agriculture. In fact, civilization began when human beings first started to practice agriculture. Before that, prehistoric people were nomadic. They wandered from place to place, hunting and fishing and eating wild nuts, grains, and berries.

Then, more than ten thousand years ago, people discovered that they could plant seeds and grow food grains. About the same time, they began to raise animals for the meat, milk, or eggs they produced. This gave early people some control over their food supply.

Planting crops and keeping domesticated animals allowed people to live in one place, rather than to wander in search of their food. These early farmers built permanent communities, which were the beginnings of civilization.

The new, settled way of life gave them time to develop new skills. They made pottery and baskets in which to store the food they harvested. People learned how to irrigate their farm land, so that their crops would have the water they needed to grow. And they learned how to make plows to cut furrows in the soil for better planting.

The greatest early civilizations of the ancient world, in Egypt and in Mesopotamia, were based on agriculture. For irrigation, the people used the waters of the Nile River in Egypt, and the Tigris and Euphrates Rivers in Mesopotamia.

Nile River

11

At first, the early farmers pulled their plows by hand. This was slow, back-breaking labor. By 3000 B.C., a new plow had been developed. The new plow made farming less difficult and more productive, because it could be pulled by oxen and guided by one person. It was faster and more efficient than the old method.

With an ox-drawn plow, farmers produced surpluses of food. The extra food

was then sold, allowing farmers to buy things they needed. The people who bought the food did not have to spend their time farming, and thus were free to do other things. They developed crafts, they mined the earth for precious stones and metals, they developed arts and learning, and they built cities. Many of the accomplishments of the ancient world were made possible by the improvements in agriculture.

14

The last great civilization of the ancient world, the Roman Empire, took farming even further. Although most Roman families grew herbs and vegetables in small kitchen gardens, relatively few citizens were full-time farmers. Farming methods were so advanced that a small number of farmers could grow enough to feed a very large, widespread population.

One of the most useful techniques to be introduced into agriculture by the Romans was two-field farming. In two-field farming, half a field was planted each year, while the other half was allowed to lie fallow, or unplanted. The portion left fallow could then recover its nutrients and moisture. By alternating farm land in this way, the Romans kept their fields fertile.

Crop rotation, terracing, and improved methods of irrigation and grain storage were other Roman contributions to agriculture. One method of crop rotation was to plant peas and beans one year and wheat the next. Beans and peas, called pulses, leave certain nutrients in the soil. Wheat, which was the foundation of the Roman diet, depended on these nutrients for growth.

Rotating peas, beans, and wheat each year.

By rotating the planting of wheat and pulses, the Romans kept their soil healthy and productive. Crop rotation is used to the same advantage in modern farming. In addition, this protects the soil against *erosion*, the wearing away of earth by wind, rain, and ground water.

Terracing is a way of using hilly land for farming. Terracing turns steep land into flat steps at different levels. These flat steps, or terraces, can be plowed and planted the same way as any other flat land. On their terraced farms, the Romans grew grapes, olives, and other fruits and vegetables. In much of Asia, where land is needed to produce food for large populations, rice is grown on hillsides on terraced farm land.

Roman technology reached a peak in the building of huge aqueducts that carried water for great distances. This made it possible for the Romans to irrigate land that would otherwise have been too dry for farming. The Romans also built excellent structures for storing grain.

The success of the Roman Empire was due in part to the Romans' ability to produce and store food. Another factor was their technological skill, which resulted in a network of roads, bridges, and aqueducts. This transportation network enabled the Romans to send food and other supplies throughout their extensive empire.

When the Roman Empire collapsed, during the fifth century A.D., agriculture in Europe changed, along with every other aspect of people's lives. In the period that followed—which was called the Middle Ages—transportation and communication between different areas came to an end.

During the Middle Ages, each small region of Europe was forced to be self-sufficient. Under a system known as feudalism, the land was divided into estates, also called manors.

Each estate was owned by a nobleman or by the church. It was farmed by peasants, known as serfs, who belonged to the estate. They were permitted to keep a small portion of what they produced, while the rest of the crops went to the lord of the manor.

Agriculture underwent a number of changes during the Middle Ages. One was the creation of the three-field system of crop rotation. Each year, in this system, two-thirds of the farm land was planted, and one-third was left fallow. In addition, different crops were planted in the two sections that were used. The next year, one of the used sections was left fallow as the system of rotation continued.

23

The introduction of a new type of harness made it possible for a horse to use its full strength when hitched to a plow. Because horses could pull a plow faster than oxen, the plowing now took less time.

Other agricultural improvements included selective breeding of plants and farm animals. This resulted in healthier, more productive strains of plants and animals.

Toward the end of the Middle Ages, two important crops—clover and turnips—were put to use by Northern European farmers. The clover added nutrients to the soil. It also made high-quality summer feed for farm animals. The turnips provided fine winter feed for the livestock.

Clover and turnips were part of a four-field rotation system that originated in England early in the eighteenth century. Turnips, clover, wheat, and another grain were planted in a four-field pattern and rotated from field to field. Each crop gave the soil nutrients that were needed by the other crops. And no land ever had to lie fallow.

The four-field rotation system produced more food for people and livestock. Meat output increased significantly. Raising sheep and cattle on a large scale became economically possible.

These advances were part of the agricultural revolution going on in Europe and North America in the eighteenth and nineteenth centuries. North America also contributed many new crops, including corn, potatoes, tomatoes, squash, and tobacco.

Cotton grew well in the American South. At first, however, it was not economical to grow, because there was no quick way to remove the seeds. Later, Eli Whitney's invention of the cotton gin solved that problem. It led to the plantation system that produced huge amounts of cotton. This was then made into cloth for clothing and other widely used products.

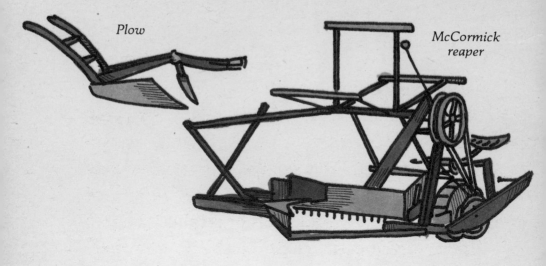

Plow

McCormick reaper

The Midwest and Plains areas of North America were ideal for growing grain on a large scale. The problem was how to plant, harvest, and thresh all this grain. The answers came from such inventions as Cyrus McCormick's reaper, the Pitts brothers' thresher, and John Deere's steel plow.

Power-driven farm machinery reduced the number of workers needed in agriculture. This replacement of workers by machinery continues today. In North

America, farms are growing larger, while the number of farm workers is growing smaller.

At the same time, the use of chemical fertilizers, herbicides, and pesticides has increased. New and hardier strains of crops have developed. These scientific contributions have helped farmers to produce more food per acre than ever before.

Agricultural researchers are constantly seeking improvements such as meatier chickens, weather- and disease-resistant varieties of rice, and faster-growing rubber trees.

In North America and Europe, there seems to be a never-ending supply and variety of food. But there are still places in the world where people go hungry. Furthermore, the world's population is growing larger every day.

As urban areas expand and more highways, housing developments, and shopping centers are built, there is less and less open land available for farming. New commercial, residential, and industrial users compete for water supplies that were formerly used primarily for irrigation of farm land. But with the help of science and space-age technology, these problems can be resolved.

And agriculture will continue to be the biggest business of all—with millions of workers sharing the vital jobs that bring our food from the farm to the table!